# From The
## *Heart*
## of The
## *Mind*

# From The *Heart* of The *Mind*

LEE ANAYA

# PALMETTO

## PUBLISHING

Charleston, SC
www.PalmettoPublishing.com



Hardcover: 979-8-8229-3847-2
Paperback: 979-8-8229-3848-9
eBook: 979-8-8229-3849-6

# In Loving Memory of Annie L. Gay

In the tapestry of my life and the verses of my heart, there exists a profound tribute to a woman of unparalleled grace and love—my late beloved Grandmother, Annie L. Gay. This collection of love poetry is a testament to her enduring presence, a melody composed from the echoes of her kindness and the warmth of her embrace.

In every stanza, I find traces of her wisdom and the gentle cadence of her laughter. Annie's spirit dances among these pages, a timeless muse who kindled the flames of my love for poetry. Though she may no longer be with us in the physical realm, her essence lingers in the verses, an eternal source of inspiration.

To my dearest Grandmother, whose love was a melody and whose life was a beautifully written poem—I dedicate this book with gratitude, love, and the everlasting imprint of your soul on mine.

With love,
Lee

## Dear Readers,

As I embark on this poetic journey with you, I am filled with a profound sense of gratitude and reflection. This collection of love poetry is not just a culmination of verses; it is a tapestry woven from the threads of life, love, and the extraordinary people who have shaped my world. In the crucible of experience, I found inspiration in the camaraderie of fellow Marines, the resilience of the human spirit, and the indomitable force that is love.

Amidst the verses that echo with the rhythm of life, I want to take a moment for special recognition, a salute to the woman whose love and strength laid the foundation for this poetic endeavor—my late and beloved Grandmother, Annie L. Gay. In the battlefield of life, she stood as a beacon of love and resilience.

This collection is not just my journey—it's a shared odyssey through love, life, and the extraordinary resilience of the human spirit. May the words within these pages stir your emotions, evoke memories, and remind you of the enduring power of love.

With heartfelt gratitude,

Lee Anaya

# A BEAUTY LIKE YOURS

How do I describe
The woman that I see
Beautiful, exquisite, angelic
Are words that come to me

Neither of us were looking
But it seems we both found it
Neither of us denying
Because there's no way around it

A beauty like yours
Is something to behold
It starts on your surface
And goes clean to your soul

You have a heated passion
That melts me to the core
Everything about you
Just makes me want you more

Lee Anaya ©2023

# A BEAUTY THAT IS MORE THAN SKIN DEEP

Beauty is only skin deep
That is what they say
But you take that statement
And simply blow it away

You have a gentleness about you
That could calm any storm
And a smile that simply radiates
Beautifully and so warm

The words that you express
Could soothe the savage beast
I know that they're effective
Because they work on me at least

A look into your eyes
A slice of Heaven to be sure
They exemplify beauty
So friendly and so pure

Your soul and your spirit
Are something to behold
They are just as beautiful
As your heart of gold

I think you're getting the point
I think I've made myself clear
The meaning of inner beauty
Is defined by you my dear

Beauty is only skin deep
Now they know it's not true
I can easily prove it
By introducing them to you

Lee Anaya ©2023

# A JOURNEY

A touch of sanity
In an insane world
A clear view
When the world is a blur
Simplicity amongst complication
A journey without destination
Climbing to the top of nowhere
To find what has not been lost
Confusing everyone
Yet making sense
Touching without hands
Speaking without words
Making an impact
Leaving an empty space behind me
Making an irrelevant difference
Winning a race never ran
Being lost in a dimension
A frame of my own mind
Confusing myself
And not knowing why
Existing in a world of hopeless reality
Reaching out
Searching
Never finding

Yet never giving up
A perverse sense of delusion
Coursing through my veins
Sending my mind into an unknown realm
Never before experienced
Crossing a new threshold
Putting me in a new frame of light
Outside of society
Yet right in the middle of it
Watching the world turn around me
Observing emotions
Watching theatrics
Carelessly thrown about
The illusions that people exist in
Afraid of reality
Living behind a mask
Afraid of the truth
Everyone heading toward suicidal destruction
Yet totally blind to it
The rules and regulations of society
Stealing our individuality
If we allow it
I do not
I deny them their satisfaction
I follow my own path

Lee Anaya © 2023

# A NEW JOURNEY

A new journey
A new path
Looking forward to the future
Learning from the past

Throw everything on the table
And we will sort it out
Anything we encounter
We will work it out

Step by step
Today by today
We will do it all together
That seems the best way

I am not going to move forward
Unless you're holding my hand
We do this as one
I know you'll understand

I hope you rest well
And sleep the night through
For while you're night dreaming of me
I'll be daydreaming of you

Lee Anaya © 2023

# AS OUR SHADOWS TOUCH

In the moon's reflection
I feel our connection
As our shadows touch

Our hearts intertwine
And so do our minds
I can definitely feel the rush

The words you speak
Are precious to me
And flow from you like gold

Feel my caress
Upon your flesh
I'm reaching for your soul

I look in your eyes
I feel my temperature rise
I love what I see

But it's not just your exterior
It's your beautiful interior
That so deeply gets to me

You whisper your words
Too softly to be heard
But I feel every one

With a subtle shift
I taste your sweet lips
I am definitely coming undone

Lee Anaya ©2023

# BECAUSE I HAVE YOU

Because I have you
My world is better
Because I have you
My thoughts are together

Because I have you
I smile a lot more
Because I have you
I'm happier than before

Because I have you
My days are so bright
Because I have you
Everything feels right

Because I have you
My sadness is gone
Because I have you
Right has replaced the wrong

Because I have you
I look forward to tomorrow
Because I have you
Happiness replaced the sorrow

I'm just so much happier
Because I have you

Lee Anaya © 2023

# BECAUSE OF YOU

My thoughts
Are all consolidated
They're simple
Definitely not complicated

My minds at peace
My hearts at rest
Beating quietly
Inside my chest

My soul is happy
Hear it sing
As I spread
My Angel wings

Now my laughter
Is so clear
And that's because
You are near

Life remains difficult
But I am calm
Just look at
What your love has done

I've found new life
I know it's true
I'm born again
Because of you

Lee Anaya © 2023

# BEYOND

Beyond description
Beyond words
Beyond Heaven
Beyond earth

Beyond beautiful
Beyond sexy
Beyond fascinating
Beyond perplexing

Beyond love
Beyond hate
Beyond destiny
Beyond fate

Beyond sight
Beyond feel
Beyond dreams
Beyond surreal

Beyond imagination
Beyond time
Beyond yours
Because she's all mine

# DON'T SETTLE FOR LESS

I'm looking for substance
I'm looking for depth
I'm looking for you
If that makes sense

A sharp wit
And cheeky banter
Are some of the things
To me that matter

You have your doubts
About yourself
But I see you
And no one else

I don't know why
Others can't see
The beautiful sunshine
That you are to me

I'll take the time
Just for you
Something others
Just won't do

Everyone has a view
For which they seek
But they won't take the effort
To climb that peak

I've seen the real you
And for that I am blessed
You're that damn good
Don't settle for less

Lee Anaya © 2023

# EVERY TIME

Beyond the realm of consciousness
That is where lies my dreams
I write the rules and regulations
So nothing is as it seems.

Join me in this fantasy
And we'll sweep the world away
Just let our emotions flow
So there will be nothing left to say

We can forget all our troubles
All our pain, anger and despair
A world where only you and I exist
Let me take you there

You will know the joy and happiness
Of the love that I have for you
We can spend forever in each other's arms
And need nothing else to do.

I have found this paradise
Yes, it exists in reality
And I experience it every time
That you are here with me.

We go beyond words
And expressions of mortal man
We go beyond the meaning of love
Every time you hold my hand.

# FALLING IN LOVE WITH YOU CAME NATURALLY

I said I would be here
And you know I meant it
Something this good
I couldn't have dreamt it

We touch and caress each other
With the words that we say
Inspiring and motivating
Every single day

But also do know
Not a word needs to be said
To understand
What's in our hearts and in our heads

An unspoken connection
Spanning time and space
Something uniquely special
That can't be replaced

We look at this crazy world
Insanity has split it open wide
But we'll make it through it all
Standing side by side

It's nothing something we tried for
It just came to be
Falling in love with you
Just came naturally

Lee Anaya ©2023

# FOR THE REST OF MY LIFE

Through difficult times
We stick together
No matter how bad
We always make it better

This isn't a race
We go at a crawl
Because we're in this together
We'll make it through it all

We make a good team
But we're much more than that
I'm not making things up
I'm simply stating facts

There are still no expectations
And we like it that way
This is how we will keep it
No matter what others say

We have finally got to meet
Together face to face
And now I really do know
No one else can take your place

You're holding my hand
Like you did on the beach
Together I know
That nothing is out of reach

Now I know what it's like
Waking up next to you
And for the rest of my life
That's what I want to do

You make the words come easy
And I thank you for that
And I know that in twenty years
All of this will still be intact 2023

Lee Anaya ©

# HEY WORLD

How do I describe
The woman that I see
Beautiful, exquisite, angelic
Are words that come to me

Neither of us were looking
But it seems we both found it
Neither of us denying
Because there's no way around it

A beauty like yours
Is something to behold
It starts on your surface
And goes clean to your soul

You have a heated passion
That melts me to the core
Everything about you
Just makes me want you more

Lee Anaya © 2023

# I WANT TO

I want to enrapture you
And capture you
I want to motivate you
And stimulate you
I want to arouse you
And astound you
I want to fill your soul
I want to make you whole
I want to adore you
I want to floor you
I want to hold you
But not control you
I want to love you
And put nothing above you
I want to kiss you
And never miss you
I want to take you
But never break you
I want to tease you
I want to please you
I want to make you mine
I want you for all time

Lee Anaya ©2023

# I WOKE UP FALLING IN LOVE WITH YOU

I woke up falling in love with you today
I really love waking up this way

All of my dreams come true
When I wake up next to you

It's really sweet you see
When my dreams become reality

In my dreams all I miss
Is the true sweetness of your kiss

In my dreams you're so beautiful
But it pales in comparison to the real you

People ask me how I slept
I say with dreams I can't forget

They say angels watch us as we sleep
My angel is laying right next to me

My heart races when I wake
Look who's next to me for Heaven's sake

I woke up smiling because all I can say
Is I woke up falling in love with you today

Lee Anaya © 2023

# I'LL NEVER UNDERSTAND

I'll never understand all your thoughts
Or some of the tears in your eyes
I may not always have the answers
But I know I'll always try

I'll never understand all your dreams
But I know you stand behind them
I will always fully support you
And help you try to find em

I'll never understand all your moods
No I won't always get it right
But I do understand this
For you I'll always fight

I'll never understand all your actions
I'll never understand all your fears
The thing I will understand
I'll always be right here

You'll never understand
Why I think you're perfect you see
I just really simply do
And that's understanding enough for me

Lee Anaya © 2023

# I'M HERE FOR YOU

Take your dreams
We will hold them together
There will never be a storm
We can't weather

I am here for you
No matter what may come
I'll be a pillar of strength
I won't come undone

Honesty and integrity
Faithfulness and trust
Those are some of the qualities
That are part of us

I want to make you smile
I want to make you laugh
I want to give you a bright future
And walk away from the past

I just want us
To have many wonderful today's
I love you and care for you
And that's all I have to say

Lee Anaya © 2023

# IF YOU WERE MINE

You're a wind through the trees
You're a song on a breeze
You're a river through a canyon
You're all I can imagine

You're a sunrise
You're a sunset
You're everything I want to remember
And nothing I want to forget

You're sweetness on my lips
And beauty to my eyes
You're every bit of wonderment
And the world's greatest surprise

You have the laughter of an angel
And full of passion and desire
You're a cool sweetness
That's filled with unquenching desire

You're definitely wonderful
You're incredibly divine
The only way you could be better
Is if you were mine

Lee Anaya © 2023

# IS WHAT YOU ARE TO ME

You are romance
You are poetry
Everything beautiful
Is what you are to me

You are my dream
You are reality
Everything fantastic
Is what you are to me

You are my future
You've everything I see
Every kind of paradise
Is what you are to me

You are my soul
The heart that beats inside of me
Such a beautiful spirit
Is what you are to me

Endless love
For eternity
Simply timeless
Is what you are to me

Lee Anaya © 2023

# IT IS

Such immensity
Such intensity
We can both feel it
It's growing stronger
It's growing longer
Some day we will reveal it

We can't tame it
Certainly can't contain it
Don't even want to try
It begins
When you breath me in
And time passes us by

Your love surrounds me
Your kiss astounds me
Like nothing ever before
I want to treasure you
I want to pleasure you
And so, so much more

You feel my touch
You feel the rush
I want to give it all to you
There's no direction
Just a deep connection
We'll be one before this is through

Lee Anaya © 2023

# IT WAS INSIDE OF YOU

I didn't create your sunshine
You did that yourself
I just moved the clouds aside
So you could shine like hell

I didn't make you an angel
I just changed your circumstance
It was inside of you
I just gave you a fighting chance

I didn't give you your smile
You created that on your own
It's a thing of beauty
Like the world has never known

I didn't give you that heart
It's all yours for real
I just held you close
And gave you time to heal

As far as your soul
That's pure perfection
Someone want to see paradise?
They can just look in your direction

The world wants to admire true beauty
Look at you and they can see
It's all your creation love
It had nothing to do with me

So when I walk with you
And people are mesmerized
It's your warm sunshine they feel
I just push the clouds aside.

Lee Anaya © 2023

# IT'S LOVE

It's complicated
It's overrated
It's anticipated
It's underrated

It's breathtaking
It's devastating
It's life changing
It's everything

It's magical
It's practical
It's radical
It's problematical

It cures your ails
Makes you feel like hell
Sometimes you can't tell
Sometimes it's just as well

It's intrusive
It's exclusive
It's conducive
It has its uses

It's productive
It's destructive
It's instructive
It's constructive

It's written about
It can be left out
It can make you shout
It can make you doubt

It will give you power
It will devour
It will leave you sour
Or be your finest hour

Everybody defines it
Everybody refines it
Some never find it
Others they don't mind it

You can feel its touch
You can feel its rush
It's what I feel for you
So damn very much

IT'S LOVE

# IT'S OUR OWN LITTLE BUBBLE

It's our own little bubble
Our own little world
I'm feeling things
I've never felt before

When our bodies connect
And you look into my eyes
I feel our soul's touch
That can't be denied

The way you look at me
When I am holding you close
Some of the most loving feelings
I have ever known

Every time we are together
We seem to learn more
Every single time
Is better than before

We are good for each other
I think that we agree
It is more than just a want
It's a heartfelt need

There will be no expectations
There will be no demands
Just a deep love for each other
Only we can understand

Lee Anaya © 2023

# IT'S SIMPLY A THOUGHT

It's like a photograph
Inside my mind
Of a different
More beautiful time

That simple thought
Makes my heart race
It takes me to
Such a magical place

So easily
It takes me away
It brings me comfort
It makes my day

I can feel it
Across my skin
I feel its embrace
As it takes me in

It heals the damage
In my soul
It's there for me
It lets me know

It's a beautiful tune
Like a favorite song
And it's there
All day long

It's a quiet whisper
You know the kind
It feels like it's making
Love to your mind

You feel it coming
When you need it most
It's like a beautiful
Invisible ghost

It makes you tingle
And you know why
That simple thought
Ignites the love inside

Indescribable
Undeniable
Always there
Always reliable

It makes you think
It makes you feel
It's what makes it
All so real

It's simply a thought
But powerful through and through
Because that simple thought
Is of you...

Lee Anaya ©2023

# IT'S YOUR LOVE
# THAT GIVES ME FAITH

I have my moments
But they quickly pass
I'll be dying inside
But just want to make you laugh

I'll always listen
When you want to vent
I don't care if I'm tired
Worn out and spent

You are my strength
And my inspiration
So you have my respect
And dedication

So why you
I've heard you ask
Because there's none better than you
And that's a fact

People see the sparkle
That's in my eye
It's from your love
I feel inside

Some have said
That I'm a good man
I just smile
Because they don't understand

I'm only half
Of what they see
The other half
Is you with me

They see
When I fall down
You pick me up
Off the ground

If I ever
Fall from grace
It's your love
That gives me faith

I learn from you
Every single day
What you do
And what you say

I'm so kind
And I'm so sweet
But without you
I'm incomplete

I'll keep it together
When you come undone
Because that's what you do
When you love someone

I will sometimes fail
Won't always succeed
But I'll give you my best
As long as I breath

Lee Anaya © 2023

# JUST A SIMPLE GESTURE

Every day I'd wake up
On the couch to the blankets in a pile
Every day I'd fold and stack them
That would always make me smile

No comment was ever made
It just simply got done
I she appreciated it
And to me it was kind of fun

I didn't do it for attention
It was just my way to say
How very much I love you
Every single day

That simple gesture was returned
I didn't have to ask
We each came up with our own
Thoughtful loving tasks

Nothing big or fancy
It doesn't have to be
Some of the simplest gestures
Mean the most you see

I came out one morning
Like I always did
But this time they weren't in a pile
And never would be again....

Just a simple gesture
Do them while you can
Because there will be a day
You'll never be able to again...

Lee Anaya © 2023

# LOOKING IN YOUR EYES

Looking in your eyes
I feel the ache
It's causing my heart to explode
And my soul to shake

It's like standing on the edge
Of today's for eternity
Standing right next to you
Preparing for sweet release

You gave me a different perspective
And I couldn't figure out why
Then it occurred to me
I'm soaring through the skies

Your touch upon my skin
Your kiss upon my lips
Now I'm realizing
What happiness is

It definitely caught me off guard
And took me by surprise
I was searching for true love
And I only had to look into your eyes

Lee Anaya ©2023

# LOVERS ARMORY

We have our armor
We have our shields
We both know
Just how we feel

Hand in hand
We take flight
Soaring together
On a starlit night

We will soar
Until daylight comes
Together we shall watch
The rising run

Together we shall hear
The angels sing
As we get lost
In our wings

And as we gently
Close our eyes
I am lost
And mesmerized

I have my Angel
Close to me
As I know
It should be

I thank you much
For who you are
The most beautiful Angel
Easily by far

Lee Anaya © 2023

# MY SOUL DANCED
# WITH YOURS TONIGHT

My soul danced with yours tonight
Lovingly, intimately, under the moonlight

As we sat there holding hands
They danced together because they understand

We're at peace once again
Our hearts opened up and let each other in

There's a comprehension that will never be heard
Because it is expressed without saying a word

I will sleep peacefully
Because I know everything will be alright

How do I know?
Because my soul danced with yours tonight

Lee Anaya © 2023

# NO MATTER HOW FAR APART

I picture you now
Letting out your sigh
Me kissing you sweetly
As you close your eyes goodnight

Another wonderful today
Because we're together in our hearts
I can feel you so close
No matter how far apart

We become more comfortable
With each other every day
We can quietly be together
Without a word to say

It grows richer
It grows stronger
We said 20 years
But it will be longer

Some things you're afraid to say
And I fully understand
I will merely love and accept
It's not my place to demand

So as you sleep my dear angel
Know one thing is very true
When you say you love me
You know I love you too

Lee Anaya © 2023

# NO SACRIFICE IS TOO STEEP

My mind races, shifting through pages
Of the book you and I have begun
The words come and go, too quickly I know
It will be a masterpiece when we are done

Inspiration and motivation, no illusion or delusion
Together we are straight and true
Together we find release, together we have peace
Despite what the world puts us through

We won't deny it, we certainly can't fight it
It wraps us in its sweet embrace
Through all of the craziness, we see through the haziness
And deep love stays in place

We are the master, through any disaster
That is just who we are
Everyone be warned, we are the perfect storm
And that will carry us far

I have looked at length, at your power and strength
I am truly mesmerized
You have your goals, this I know
You refuse to be denied

There are times when you're confused, maybe feeling
used
But I will not let you down
No matter what storm comes, I will not run
I will firmly stand my ground

Lee Anaya © 2023

# NOW AND FOREVER

She's in my soul
I breath her in
She's in my blood
She is on my skin

She is in my thoughts
She influences them
She is in my consciousness
My demons, she gets me through them

She changed my life
I will never be the same
She is in my soul
She is in my veins

She is my existence
I have no resistance
I feel her power
Through my soul

That I could be this happy
I never knew

Take me completely
Now and forever
Time will end but this will never

Lee Anaya © 2023

# NOW FOR THE FUTURE

I think of the times we've had
And of the times that could be
I try to look into the future
And am unsure of what I see

I know not what lies ahead
But I know what we have been through
If there is a future for us
It lies between me and you

My love for you is undying
As time has surely shown
I thought that time would wear it away
But it has only grown

I thought I had known happiness
And it seemed to be with me all along
But when I first held you in my arms
I realized then that I was wrong

I have fought long and hard for you
And eventually I hope to win
And even against all the odds
I never will give in

As time will fade away
My love for you will grow
But what the future holds for both of us
Only time can know

Lee Anaya © 2023

# NOW UNTIL ETERNITY

There's a wall in front of me
You know that I will break through
I will keep on climbing
Because I can't wait to see the view

I'm looking towards the future
Trying to keep you from the past
From now until eternity
Is how long I'm going to last

I know you have your insecurities
I know you have your doubts
But every single day
I will wipe them out

You are worth the wait
And definitely worth the fight
I'm going to take this slowly
I'm going to do this right

Each day we feel closer
I know that you do too
I'm in this for the long run
I will see this through

Lee Anaya © 2023

# OUR LOVE

Like a reed bent in the wind
That grows back with the sun
And the rain
Our love shall always be there
To carry us further
And always "we" shall remain

We shall not falter
Neither shall we fail
For through our common love
And understanding
We shall always prevail

Through our communication
Whether by body or by word
The messages we give to each other
Shall always clearly be heard

Every road that you shall follow
And every path that you shall stride
Every time you turn around
I will be there by your side

The love and adoration you bestow upon me
Is something I find totally new
I am hopelessly in love with you babe
And there's nothing that I can do

As time will pass us by
And the years go on their way
I know that we shall remain together
Until our dying day.......

Lee Anaya ©2023

# PARADISE

Sssshhhhh
Don't say a word
Let's leave this peace
Completely undisturbed

I just know
That you can hear it
It's paradise
And we're oh so near it

Don't rush
Take it slow
Because our hearts
Know exactly where to go

Close your eyes
We don't need to speak
Listen to our souls
They know what they seek

Listen to the music
We know the tune
That's our hearts beating
They know what's coming soon

Our bodies connect
As our lips touch
Take your time
There's no need to rush

The moon will be shining
Upon us all night
We know we waited
Until the time was right

When the sun says good morning
I know one thing for sure
There's no doubt
My heart will be yours

Lee Anaya ©2023

# PROMISES OF TOMORROW

Take my hand in yours
And feel the beat of my heart
Feel us getting closer
And never drifting apart

Look deeply in my eyes
And you'll never see sorrow
You'll only see happiness
And promises of tomorrow

Let me hold you
Tightly in my arms
Protecting you from sadness
And anything that harms

Softly kiss my lips
Feel my love for you
For it shall truly endure
Until time is through

Lee Anaya © 2023

# ROSES IN THE EVENING

Roses in the evening
Being kissed by the moon
Oh how I yearn
To be with you soon

Each one of them spoke to me
Calling out your name
Touching my heart so deeply
Knowing you feel the same

The rose bushes beauty
Whether alone or as a group
No matter how they try
Can't compare to you

I catch their scent
They surely smell so sweet
But if they competed with you
They'd definitely face defeat

Roses in the evening
Nature thank you for your time
But when it comes to beautiful flowers
None can compare to mine

Lee Anaya © 2023

# SHE IS

She's a whisper in a windstorm
A cool breeze when it's too warm
A perfect combination

She's the twinkle in the starlight
Gentle shade when it's too bright
She's beyond imagination

She's a cool drink for my parched soul
The easy answers for what I don't know
She makes me a better man

Her heart is pure love
She fits me like a silk glove
She's the one that understands

She's the passion in my dreams
She's everything it seems
I wouldn't want her to be any other way

She's what fits between the lines
What really fits is her soul and mine
And there's nothing else to say

Lee Anaya © 2023

# SHE'S

She makes an impression
That's beyond expression
She simply leaves me breathless
There's no denying
That without even trying
She makes my heart so restless

There's no need for explanation
She's my favorite destination
Where all my dreams travel to
She's beauty to the soul
And it protects her heart of gold
She's amazing through and through

She's the epitome of strength
And oh so many other things
But her feet are firmly on the ground
She's always so humble
And even when she stumbles
She's classy all around

She's beauty and she's magic
She's calmness through the tragic
You better mind your p's and q's
Here's a gentle reminder
Don't look because you won't find her
Until she's ready for you

Always remember her you won't forget her
You're good she'll make you better
She's an angel upon this earth
And don't you ever disrespect her
Because I am here to protect her
And I damn well know what she is worth

Lee Anaya © 2023

# SINCE THE DAY I MET YOU

You have an incredible inner strength
And an incredible inner core
You give all that you have
Then you give a little more

You've been through a lot in life
And yet you persevere
You do well hiding your doubts
And hiding most of your fears

You don't do well with compliments
And in person you claim you're shy
And try to ignore the beauty
That you simply cannot hide

Yes, we really love each other
But seriously can't you see
I mean the compliments I give
And not just because of what you mean to me

Since the day I met you
I wanted the world to know
The amazing woman you are
And I wanted it to show

I don't give empty praise
And I don't say things just because
I mean everything I say
That's what a gentleman does

I've never written poems
The way you inspire me to
It's just that poetry comes easy
When describing a woman like you

Lee Anaya ©2023

# SOMEDAY

Someday you'll learn
That my words are true
I don't say them
To please or appease you

I love you and respect you
So, I hope that It's plain you see
That you're a very beautiful woman
And it's not just me

You're shy and beautiful and bashful
And don't take compliments well
But I very sincerely mean them
Look in my eyes and you can tell

Not just my words
But my actions say the same
That I'm serious about you
It's not just a game

My poems for you
Are because of who you are
How close we feel to each other
Even though the distance is so far

I love your kiss
I love your touch
You know everything about you
I really love so much

Lee Anaya © 2023

# THANK YOU

Thank you for loving me
Thank you for caring
Thank you for wanting me
Thank you for sharing

Thank you for being beautiful
Inside and out
Thank you for having my back
And leaving no doubt

Thank you for being something else
Like no one else on earth
Thank you for enjoying your life with me
And knowing what it's worth

Thank you for being an incredible woman
And surviving all the mess
Thank you for the extra sunshine in my life
And putting at ease the stress

Thank you for our chats

Without knowing how we got to here from there
Thank you for the most wonderful laughs
That you and I share

Thank you for playing along
When I'm bold and a little crass
Thank you for being patient
When I'm really being an ass

Thank you for needing me
And everything we go through
Thank you for holding my hand and my heart
And never letting go

Lee Anaya ©

# THE ONE

As each day goes by my love
No matter what we may go through
For the rest of my life
This is what I promise to you
I promise to be
The one who will dry your tears
And kiss away the pain
The one who is your umbrella
For every time it rains
The one who causes you to smile
For simply no reason at all
The one who appreciates your accomplishments
No matter how big or small
The one who holds you close
In the middle of the night
The one who makes you feel better
When nothing is going right
The one who wakes up next to you
Each and every day
The one who fills you with the words
When you don't know what to say
The one who helps you create a whole new world

Full of joy and happiness
The one who will always hold you
With love and tenderness
The one who never asks too much of you
Is neither pushy or demanding
The one who always offers you
Patience and understanding
The one who will need you
And want you more each day
The one who shall always love you
More than words can say
The one who gives you pleasure
Of body, heart and mind
And most of all, I promise to love you
Until the end of time

Lee Anaya © 2023

# THE WAY YOU MAKE ME FEEL

I look at your pictures
And I look in your eyes
The way that you look at me
Still takes me by surprise

Your eyes are so beautiful
Loving and warm
You look at me in a way
Like I haven't been looked at before

I know you don't believe it
But I fall in love with you every day
If anything of this becomes too much
Please don't hesitate to say

I can't help myself
The way you make me feel
Sometimes it feels like a dream
Like this is all surreal

But the moment that I first held your hand
Or kissed your soft, sweet lips
I knew love
I knew this was it

Am I seeing something
That really isn't there?
If I was, I know you'd tell me
Because I know you really care

So, I will continue
To let my heart and mind race
The way it always does
Every time I see your face

Lee Anaya © 2023

# THERE'S SIMPLY NO DENYING

I reach for words
But they elude me
Your beautiful eyes
See right through me

Your gentle caress
Upon my skin
Opened my heart
And you walked right in

I feel your love so deep
And it surrounds me
There are reminders of you
All around me

This is innocent and pure
So deep and so real
I can't wait for each day with you
And what it reveals

We found each other
Without even trying
We are falling for each other
There's simply no denying

Lee Anaya © 2023

# TOGETHER AND ALONE

The beautiful glow of your face
Could remove the moon and take its place
The beautiful sparkle in your eyes
Could replace the stars in the sky

I want to hold you close
Feel your body next to mine
Get lost in the paradise
I know that we could find

Kiss your lips so softly
And listen to you moan
We finally have that moment
Together and alone

Let me make sweet love to you
I want you to feel my touch
Take my time and go all night
Something too good to rush

Let me look into your beautiful eyes
As we become one
The sun will rise and set
Before our pleasure is done

Lee Anaya © 2023

# TOGETHER

I see your words
Come across the screen
An amazing beauty
Rarely seen

There's a deep connection
That we share
Read our words
You'll find it there

We communicate
With words unspoken
Our souls have a bond
That can never be broken

We have shared many moments
That to others will remain unknown
Intimately, intellectually
Together we have grown

We've touched each other in ways
That the rest of them couldn't
We've been there for each other
In ways that others wouldn't

We've shared the heat
And kept each other warm
Our hearts and souls connect
Making the perfect storm

You opened yourself up
And let me in
I'll never see beauty
Like yours again

We love and we cherish
What we write and what we say
Our love and respect
Will remain for every today

Lee Anaya © 2023

# TOTALLY DEDICATED

Totally dedicated
Totally committed
One hundred percent
I am in it

I don't care
What others have done
I have no fear
I will not run

Whatever they've done
Pass on to me
I want our future clear
Don't you see

You have a past
But don't we all
No one is perfect
I do recall

I'm not afraid
Put me to the test
I want to lay your fears
To final rest

Let's look forward
Our future is clear
I don't care
What's in the mirror....

Lee Anaya © 2023

# UNDERSTANDING EACH OTHER

Understanding each other
Through words unspoken
Long sleeping romance
Quietly awoken

Our hearts were wondering aimlessly
But we found a connection
Now they're blissfully traveling
In the same direction

Every day it seems
We're discovering something new
Every sunrise is beautiful
Because I wake up to you

You are poetry in motion
You are poetry itself
You make me feel
Unlike I've ever felt

A definition for you
Simply doesn't exist
Even Cupid couldn't create
A love such as this

I really try to personify
The meaning of romance
Because against you
I don't stand a chance

I can't wait to see
What happens next
You keep me guessing
And beautifully perplexed

No matter what the future holds
We know we have it covered
Because we're simply
Understanding each other

Lee Anaya ©2023

# UNTIL YOU COME BACK

I listen to my heartbeat
Without a sound
It's always empty
When you're not around

It slows down
Then just goes quiet
It's crazy about you
I simply can't deny it

It patiently waits
For the sound of your voice
Then it can be happy
Then it can rejoice

When you are near
It's a real powerhouse
But when you're gone
It's quiet as a mouse

As you softly sleep
It quietly waits
Holding itself together
Trying not to break

Until you come back
And I know that you will
It will just sit here
Quiet and still....

Lee Anaya © 2023

# WE ARE LOVE

We are love
We are romance
We are something special
Because we gave this a chance

We are beautiful poetry written
We are everything to be
Just watch us for a bit
And you will definitely see

We are amazing happiness
We are joyful laughter
We are private jokes
And everything hereafter

We are wonderful music
We're a kind of magic
We are more
Then anyone could imagine

We are a wonderful today
We're the hopes for tomorrow
We are a kind of happiness
Everyone wants to borrow

Want to know
How we made it this far
One simple explanation
We simply are

Lee Anaya © 2023

# WE HAVE US

The words are there
They are easy to say
The depth of your love
Makes it that way

Some of our words go unspoken
But all of our promises remain unbroken
Our strength lies within

Persistent against resistance
Our love is consistent
And we will never give in

So many others envy us
Because they know they can't be us
No matter how hard they try

Sometimes we have an uphill climb
Something neither of us minds
Because we simply won't be denied

We have been through hell and fire
But side by side we are inspired
That's what makes us succeed

I have your heart and you have mine
A deeper love you will never find
Each other is all we need

Thank you today, tomorrow and evermore
Your love is like nothing I've seen before
And will never see again

We have love and adoration
Respect and admiration
We are lifetime love and forever friends

We have each other's back
There's nothing that we lack
We've got it covered day and night

We have honesty and trust
Most importantly we have us
And there's nothing left to write

Lee Anaya © 2023

# WHAT CAN I SAY

I journey through a realm
That to me, before was unknown
It was a place of dreams
Where never a seed was sown

I knew it existed but I let it be
For in there fear I had found
I tried to walk across the plain
Only to be thrown to the ground

Many times, I talked about it
And wrote poems for it galore
It was a dream, a fantasy
All of that and nothing more

I journeyed through hatred, despair and pain
Begging for a release
I could feel the torture wearing me down
And wishing that it would cease

I went from one relationship to another
Thinking that I could never be tamed
But wishing deep in my heart
That it would not always be the same

But then one day there was a knocking
A knocking on my door
And crashing through all of my walls
Was a beauty that I had not seen before

You were a beckoning light
An answer to all of my needs
You were the one I had waited for
And this I firmly believed

You didn't wait for permission
You just stole my heart away
You took and returned love
And there was nothing for me to say

A hole was filled and memories erased
All in the blink of an eye
And before I knew what was happening
There was a "You and I"

Your love struck me down
And tied up my heart
But who was I to complain
Your love was so strong
And I knew from the start
That things would never be the same

Now I grasp for words
Words that I might say
To let you know how I feel
But words just aren't enough
To bring it across
To show you my love is real

What I want to say is what you make me feel
I have never felt before
Because it is now you babe
That I love and adore

Lee Anaya © 2023

# WHAT SHE IS

I look so deeply in her eyes
She's more beautiful than she might realize
Her heart, her mind, her soul, her face
Not a single damn thing would I replace
Let my eyes be your mirror to see
Just how much you mean to me
A million memories in my mind
A million more for us to find
Dirt roads, paved, roads, and even cobblestone
I want to walk all roads, with you and you alone
The wind whispers our names
The rain sings our son
Even mother nature it seems
Knows that we belong
The first day you smiled at me
Set everything in motion
Our souls connecting deeply
As one in true and dear devotion
It doesn't matter what life brings
Or what we have to go through
I don't care what tomorrow holds
Because yesterday brought me you

Lee Anaya ©2023

# WHEN IT'S MEANT TO BE

I just got off the phone with you
And of course, my mind races
So many things we want to do together
And see so many places

Wordlessly we connect
Through our hearts and minds
And we make a future together
Leaving the bad of the past behind

It's a natural fit
Of that we have both agreed
To rush or to explain things
There simply is no need

I know the warmth of holding your hand
I know the sweetness of your kiss
There are more intimate things we will enjoy
There's nothing we will miss

Everything will happen
When it's meant to be
Each today that we face
What happens we will just see

There's no analyzing
Just acceptance of what comes
But we will journey a lifetime together
Before this is done

Lee Anaya ©

# WHEN YOU REALLY LOVE SOMEONE

I see you with my heart and mind
And neither of them has eyes
They both think you're beautiful
I hope you realize

When you really love someone
By now you should have guessed
I'm I love with your heart and mind
I'm not worried about the flesh

My hands will caress your curves
And I will taste your lips
I want a taste of Heaven
And my love you are definitely it

Your laughter to me is ageless
And your smile never tires
Every time I see your eyes
They always have that fire

When it comes time
For us to interact
I find you desirable
It's a plain and simple fact

And whenever you hold my hand
My heart simply skips a beat
When it comes to beauty
You have everything I need

You have my heart and soul
Don't ever let them go
And when it comes to my eyes
They're only for you, you know

Lee Anaya © 2023

# WHO YOU ARE

You're simply the most beautiful woman
That I have known by far
It's not just how you look
But also who you are

I love your sweet lips
And your beautiful eyes
But there's more to you
Than most people realize

You're beautiful and caring
You're loving and sweet
And I'll be damned
If you don't have the cutest little feet

You're smile and laughter
I want until the hereafter
And your voice gently lingers
Like the sweet touch of your fingers

Your heart is genuine gold
Just like your beautiful soul
You're smart and you're witty
Gorgeous and so pretty

This poem is unconventional
But then again at times so are you
So I'll phrase it simply
Damn I very much love you

Lee Anaya © 2023

# WINDS FROM THE SEA

As we walk along the beach
Our feet sliding through the sand
Thought we're walking side by side
I wish we were walking hand in hand

Our conversation flows lightly
Like the winds from the sea
But despite the chill I feel
I sense your warmth next to me

I love to hear you laugh
And I love to see you smile
They make the moments alone with you
All the more worthwhile

Though the moon is hidden away
The beach is glowing bright
And I know it's from the woman
Who is walking on my right

The beauty you possess
Seems to overwhelm me
A beauty from without and within
It's truly plain to see

I look at you and see you smile
And I yearn to hold you near
I want to softly kiss your lips
But I'm being restrained by fear

I feel something when we're alone
Tell me, do you feel it too?
Please express your thoughts to me
Tell me what I do to you

I don't want to push
I know want to know
Don't hold anything back
Let it all go

I hold nothing against you
And you have nothing to fear from me
Come, take my hand, hold me close
And feel how good it can be....

Lee Anaya ©

# YOU

You amaze me and astound me
You help me soar and you ground me

You give me love and desire
You give me sweetness and fire

You give passion and laughter
And wanting you forever after

You give me calm and peace
You give my heart sweet release

You give me food for my soul
You give me more than you will ever know

You give me guidance in a world of doubt
When I feel trapped you help me out

You give me beauty to find
When I feel myself lost and blind

You give me truth and honesty
After what the world has done to me

You give me loving help
When I make a mistake and can't forgive myself

You tell me what I need to hear
Not just what I want like others I fear

You never mess with my mind or play games
You are always rock solid, always the same

You're priceless and precious
Your love is addictive and infectious

Your smile is love revealing
Your heart gives me cherished healing

You have some wisdom and wit
Our love just seems to fit

YOU, hell, just doesn't get any better

Lee Anaya © 2023

# YOU'RE SIMPLY YOU

How clearly I see your elegance
How clearly I see your grace
And the incredible beauty
Of your sweet face

I feel your kindness
And how sweet you can be
But I also see your strength
And deep ferocity

You're a beautiful poem
And a sweet love song
You're incredible fairness
Even though you've been wronged

You're intelligence and wisdom
And amazing creativity
You're definitely an example
Of how good someone can be

You're the sweetness of a kiss
The softness of a touch
You're the one
That gives my heart such a rush

You're happiness and joy
Truly fulfilled
You're incredible beauty
Gently revealed

You're so many things
That's very true
The most amazing of all
Is that you're simply you

Lee Anaya © 2023

# YOUR MOONLIGHT

You like the darkness
I will be your moonlight
Under the stars
Everything will be right

We both feel the pull
It's definitely magnetic
The blending of our words
Beautifully poetic

No expectations
Completely surprised
You could sense it
Slowly arise

New and refreshing
Innocent and pure
Magically beautiful
Of that we're sure

I'll sit here tonight
Lost in thoughts of you
And at sunrise
We will begin anew

Thank you for the kindness
You've shown to me
Take my hand in yours
No telling just what could be

Lee Anaya © 2023